JERRI WOOD

PURSUE

THE LAMB

Pursue the Lamb
Copyright © 2025 by Jerri Wood

ISBN: 979-8998742453 (sc)
ISBN: 979-8998742460 (e)

Riverview Press

info@riverview-press.com
www.riverview-press.com

Revelation 5: 6 and 14

Then I saw a Lamb, looking as if it had been slain, standing in the center before the throne, encircled by the four living creatures and elders.

The four living creatures said, "Amen," and the elders fell down and worshiped.

Acknowledgements

I would like to take time to mention all the wonderful people who made this book possible.

First, there are the ladies of Rockbridge Church of God Holiness who made it possible to get this book published.

Pat Ravenscraft who took the time to read each and every one of these devotions and gave me feedback.

Judy Woltz who read each devotion for me and gave me honest opinions.

Stephanie Remington, my daughter, who is my graphic artist. She put together my cover front and back.

To my husband for once again being willing to support me as I write.

To my publisher, Rosemary Fisher with Riverview Press. Without her this book would not be a reality.

Thank you one and all. You are truly the greatest!

Contents

A New Day

Ephesians 1:17-19 ESV

That the God of our Lord Jesus Christ, the Father of glory, may give you the Spirit of wisdom and of revelation in the knowledge of him, having the eyes of your hearts enlightened, that you may know what is the hope to which he has called you, what are the riches of his glorious inheritance in the saints, and what is the immeasurable greatness of his power toward us who believe, according to the working of his great might.

These are the things Paul prayed for the Ephesians.

That God would give them the Spirit of wisdom and revelation, to know Him better.

1. The eyes of their hearts would be enlightened.

2. They would know the hope to which He has called them.

3. For the riches of His glorious inheritance.

4. To know His incomparably great power.

Wow! What if we prayed for these same things for ourselves? What if we prayed them for other people? What a change we would see in our lives and our churches.

Let's give it a try and see what God has for us. Maybe you could choose a couple of people to pray for in this way and see what happens! It's a good way to start a new day!

Pursue the Lamb

Romans 15:5-6

May the God who gives endurance and encouragement give you the same attitude of mind toward each other that Christ Jesus had, so that with one mind and one voice you may glorify the God and Father of our Lord Jesus Christ.

Ephesians 3:7

I became a servant of this gospel by the gift of God's grace given me through the working of his power.

Colossians 1:28

We proclaim him, admonishing and teaching everyone with all wisdom, so that we may present everyone fully mature in Christ.

Chase the King

Psalm 24:8

Who is this King of Glory? The LORD strong and mighty, the LORD mighty in battle.

I read this phrase, "Chase the King," and I haven't been able to get it out of my mind. It was one of the first things I thought after watching the play, "David", at Sight and Sound.

It dawned on me that King David did just this very thing for most of his life! Think about how he started out.

First, he was a shepherd for years, spending lots of time with his sheep, alone in the hills where he had a lot of time to talk to God and make his music. He was talking to God, looking for answers to questions, gaining wisdom-chasing the King.

Then as he moved from field to palace, he played his lyre for a madman. He needed God's guidance and His protection. I'm sure there were moments when he pursued his King, in order to be safe.

As he became king himself and had to go into battle after battle, God's protection became even more important. Then came the BIG HICCUP where David forgot to chase the King, but you know what- God then chased him. The tables were turned until David came back to right.

Because David chased the King, he was called a man after God's own heart. You know the rest of the story. But what about you? Are you chasing the King?

When you chase after something you intend to catch it! Find out what the Father wants from you. Look to Him, fix your eyes on Jesus, worship Him, praise Him, love Him, come before Him with singing. Let the King permeate your very being. Don't let another day go by. Chase the King.

Pursue the Lamb

1 Samuel 16:18

One of the servants answered, "I have seen a son of Jesse of Bethlehem who knows how to play the lyre. He is a brave man and a warrior. He speaks well and is a fine-looking man. And the LORD is with him.

1 Samuel 16:19

Then Saul sent messengers to Jesse and said, "Send me your son David, who is with the sheep."

Acts 13:22

After removing Saul, he made David their king. God testified concerning him; "I have found David son of Jesse, a man after my own heart; he will do everything I want him to do."

Just Say the Word

Matthew 8:8

The centurion replied, "Lord, I do not deserve to have you come under my roof. But just say the word, and my servant will be healed."

The centurion was concerned about his servant. The man was very sick. He needed a touch from Jesus and the centurion knew Who to ask. One interesting part of this story is that this military officer was a Roman. He wasn't a Jewish follower, but he was obviously aware of Jesus' reputation.

Because this man oversaw other men, he had a unique way of interacting with Jesus. He knew Jesus was in authority over nature, sickness and spirits. He had enough faith, that he believed Jesus could heal from afar.

Guess what? That's exactly what happened! Because Jesus just "said the word", the centurion's servant was healed.

How about you? Are you needing Jesus to just "say the word" about some situation you are dealing with? Some wayward child, a marriage in trouble, a financial need, what about an unplanned pregnancy? He can take care of that for you, you know? Amaze Jesus with your faith (Matthew 8:10) and watch what He will do.

Pursue the Lamb

Psalm 107:19-20

Then they cried to the LORD in their trouble, and he saved them from their distress. He sent out his word and healed them; he rescued them from the grave.

Matthew 15:28

Then Jesus said to her, "Woman, you have great faith! Your request is granted." And her daughter was healed from that very hour.

Matthew 9:22

Jesus turned and saw her. "Take heart, daughter," he said, "your faith has healed you." And the woman was healed from that moment.

Who is God to You?

Read Psalm 62:5-8

Yes, my soul, find rest in God;
  my hope comes from him.
⁶ Truly he is my rock and my salvation;
  he is my fortress, I will not be shaken.
⁷ My salvation and my honor depend on God;
  he is my mighty rock, my refuge.
⁸ Trust in him at all times, you people;
  pour out your hearts to him,
  for God is our refuge.

How do you view God? Is he some other-worldly being, just waiting to zap you with a lightning bolt for doing some perceived wrong? Or is He more of a father figure to you? Whether He is either one of these things, or somewhere in between, this Bible passage today gives us a perspective on God's character that brings hope.

Just look at all the nouns that are listed in those four verses: Rest, Salvation, Rock, Fortress, Hope, Mighty Rock, Refuge. Let this list soak into your soul for a moment. Do you need strength? Stand on the Rock. Do you need hope? Put your faith in the Savior.

These are just a few verses with just a few characteristics of who God can be for you. Are you trusting Him today to be your Rock? Maybe you need a Refuge in which to run. Or maybe you just need to come to Him and rest. At any rate, when you seek Him, you WILL find Him. Don't quit until you do!

Pursue the Lamb

Psalm 37:5-6

Commit your way to the LORD; trust in him and he will do this: He will make your righteous reward shine like the dawn, your vindication like the noonday sun.

Psalm 42:4

These things I remember as I pour out my soul; how I used to go to the house of God under the protection of the Mighty One with shouts of joy and praise among the festive throng.

Psalm 61:3

For you have been my refuge, a strong tower against the foe.

Psalm 33:20-21

We wait in hope for the LORD; he is our help and our shield. In him our hearts rejoice, for we trust in his holy name. May your unfailing love be with us, LORD, even as we put our hope in you.

Jehovah My Song

Isaiah 12:2 KJV

Behold, God is my salvation; I will trust and not be afraid; for the LORD Jehovah is my strength and my song; he is also become my salvation.

God is my strength and my song! The NIV says the LORD is my strength and my defense.

Do you ever get a song stuck in your head? That happens to me a lot! Sometimes that song will be there for days, to the point that I must sing a different song just to get it out of there!

I found it interesting in this scripture that one version says God is my song and another says God is my defense. I'm thinking just maybe I get those songs get stuck in my head to help me keep my mind on the One who is my salvation. God has given me a song so I can stay on the right track of always keeping Him in the forefront of my mind.

What a great God we have, that He even gives us a song as a defense. It helps us draw closer to Him. If we are singing about Him or to Him, we can't really be off track and have our thoughts on wrong things. Isn't it amazing the things God does for us and we don't even realize it? Sing those songs for all you are worth! God loves to hear you singing about Him.

Pursue the Lamb

Psalm 26:1

Vindicate me, LORD, for I have led a blameless life; I have trusted in the LORD and have not faltered.

Psalm 96:1

Sing to the LORD a new song; sing to the LORD, all the earth. Sing to the LORD, praise his name, proclaim his salvation day after day.

Revelation 5:9

And they sang a new song, saying: "You are worthy to take the scroll and open its' seals, because you were slain, and with your blood you purchased for God members of every tribe and language and people and nation."

Cast Your Cares

Psalm 55:22

Cast your cares on the LORD and he will sustain you; he will never let the righteous be shaken.

When I see the word, "cast," I get a mental image of a fisherman sending his line flying out over the water or a person throwing something away from themselves with some force behind it.

If we cast or throw our cares on the Lord, our promise today is that He will sustain us.

He will keep us. He will hold us up. He will strengthen us during those trials that come our way.

The very best part of this verse comes toward the end. God will *never* ever let the righteous be shaken. Will bad things come our way? Most likely. Does that mean we stop believing that God is good? I hope not! I recently went to a conference where I heard this: There are two pillars we should live between. The first is that God is good, and the other is that God is powerful. If we live between these two things and we pray believing these things, we will be sustained!

Read verse 22 again. His promise is that He *will sustain* us. He will *not* let us be shaken. Cast your cares on Him. He can handle it!

Pursue the Lamb

1 Peter 5:7

Cast all your anxiety on him because he cares for you.

Psalm 37:5-6

Commit your way to the LORD, trust in him and he will do this: He will make your righteous reward shine like the dawn, your vindication like the noonday sun.

Psalm 18:6

In my distress I called to the LORD; I cried to my God for help. From his temple he heard my voice; my cry came before him, into his ears.

Psalm 68:19

Praise be to the LORD, to God our Savior, who daily bears our burdens.

The Transformed

Mark 9:2 NLT

Six days later Jesus took Peter, James, and John, and led them up a high mountain to be alone. As the men watched, Jesus' appearance was transformed.

Undoubtedly, you've seen or heard about transformers. If you haven't, walk down the toy aisle at the department store or look them up on a movie channel. Transformers go from being a car, truck or some other form of transportation, to being this huge mechanical being that is powerful and does all kinds of amazing things.

In the Bible it tells of Jesus who was transformed. No, He didn't turn into a mechanical being! Instead, right there on that mountain Jesus was changed into a more beautiful being! Right before the eyes of some of his disciples. (2 Pet. 1:16-18). When He was transformed his clothing became bright white and his face shone like the sun!

Jesus was transformed in his physical appearance, and He does that same work through us. He is always working on our heart and mind, helping us to be more beautiful for Him, transforming us into His image. In the end, He will elevate us to our place in heaven, when we have put our trust in Him and Him alone. Let Jesus transform you today. You won't regret it!

Pursue the Lamb

Romans 12:2

Do not conform to the pattern of this world, but be transformed by the renewing of your mind. Then you will be able to test and approve what God's will is - his good, pleasing and perfect will.

2 Corinthians 3:18

And we all, who with unveiled faces contemplate the Lord's glory, are being transformed into his image with ever increasing glory, which comes from the Lord, who is the Spirit.

Philippians 3:21

Who by the power that enables him to bring everything under his control, will transform our lowly bodies so that they will be like his glorious body.

Creator of Earth

Isaiah 40:28

Do you not know? Have you not heard? The LORD is the everlasting God, the Creator of the ends of the earth.

When you look at our earth what do you see? There are so many amazing things in nature. Think about the mountains and the rainforests and oceans and all the different species of animals. The way everything interacts with nature is amazing, too. All animals are made to be in the exact environment in which they live.

Do you know why? Because God ordained it to be that way! He is the Creator of the ends of the earth. He is GOD! He is sovereign. He made all this earth that we call home. He didn't make any mistakes when He did it.

He made you too. And guess what? He didn't make a mistake there either! You are exactly who He meant you to be. When you accept Him, He takes who you are and works with you so you can bring glory to Him.

He is the everlasting God; He loves you more than words can say. He is the Creator of the ends of the earth. Get out today and enjoy this beautiful earth He created for you! Praise Him today.

Pursue the Lamb

Psalm 90:2

Before the mountains were born or you brought forth the whole world, from everlasting to everlasting you are God.

Genesis 1:24

And God said, "Let the land produce living creatures according to their kinds, livestock, creatures that move along the ground and wild animals, each according to its kind." And it was so.

Genesis 1:27

So God created human beings in his own image, in the image of God he created them; male and female he created them.

Isaiah 37:16

LORD Almighty, the God of Israel, enthroned between the cherubim, you alone are God over all the kingdoms of the earth. You have made heaven and earth.

Salvation

Acts 4:12

Salvation is found in no one else, for there is no other name given under heaven by which we must be saved.

There is only one name we can call on to be saved. Salvation is found in no one else. What is that name? Jesus Christ the Son of God! Salvation means that we are free from sin. How do we get to the place in our life where we can feel that freedom?

Here is shortened version of how to accept Jesus:

1. Repent- recognize that you are a sinner, tell God you know that you have sinned in your life.

2. Believe- believe that Jesus died for you and that He is God's Son.

3. Confess- tell God you are sorry for the wrong things you have done and ask Him to forgive you.

4. Receive- accept that He has done what you have asked. Take this salvation as a free gift. Then turn from those wrongs and start to live for Him.

As you can see, it really is a pretty simple thing to do. God doesn't expect us to be perfect, just forgiven. Salvation is very important because it is the only way to spend eternity with Jesus! Make that commitment today.

Pursue the Lamb

Matthew 1:21

She will give birth to a son, and you are to give him the name Jesus, because he will save his people from their sins.

John 14:6

Jesus answered: "I am the way and the truth and the life. No one comes to the Father except through me."

I Timothy 2:6

For there is one God and one mediator between God and human beings. Christ Jesus, himself human, who gave himself as a ransom for all people. This has now been witnessed to at the proper time.

Prayer of Repentance:

Dear Jesus,

I come before you now asking for your help. Please forgive me for the things I've done in this life that are wrong, for my sins. I confess that I have not done the things You consider to be right. I believe that You died for me. Please forgive me and help me now to receive this free gift You've given me. In Your name, Jesus. Amen.

Justification

Acts 13:38-39

Therefore, my friends, I want you to know that through Jesus the forgiveness of sins is proclaimed to you. Through him everyone who believes is set free from every sin, a justification you were not able to obtain under the law of Moses.

I once heard the word justification defined like this: "It's just as if I'd never sinned." Isn't that a wonderful thought? That is what it means. Once Jesus has forgiven you of your sins, it's like they were never there!

When Christ came, he made a way through his death and resurrection for us to be made clean. If we are willing and accept Jesus, we can be free from sin. He wipes out what we have done in our past and doesn't hold any of it against us! It's just as if we'd never sinned!

Am I saying that God just acts like everything is all good between us and Himself? Yes, that's exactly what I'm saying. We cannot make ourselves clean, good, or right in God's sight. Only Jesus can do that for you. If He has forgiven you, then those sins are cast as far as the east is from the west!

Our verse says that we by ourselves and our rules and laws could never have attained freedom from sin. We had to have Jesus to make us right in God's sight. I'm thankful we can be free through faith in our Savior. God worked on our behalf because we were never going to be able to attain this by ourselves. Trust Him today to take care of those sins and make you clean!

Pursue the Lamb

Romans 3:23-24

For all have sinned and fall short of the glory of God, and all are justified freely by his grace through the redemption that came by Christ Jesus.

Luke 24:47

And repentance for the forgiveness of sins will be preached in his name to all nations, beginning at Jerusalem.

Acts 2:38

Peter replied, "Repent and be baptized, every one of you, in the name of Jesus Christ for the forgiveness of your sins. And you will receive the gift of the Holy Spirit.

Psalm 103:11-12

For as high as the heavens are above the earth, so great is his love for those who fear him; as far as the east is from the west, so far has he removed our transgressions from us.

Reconciliation

2 Corinthians 5:18

All this is from God who reconciled us to himself through Christ and gave us the ministry of reconciliation.

Reconciliation happens when two people who were previously enemies come back together and establish peace between themselves.

That's what Jesus did for us when he came to earth. You see, we humans were far from God. There was sin that stood between us and him. The only person who could have ever made the sacrifice for us was Jesus. He came here and lived among us, so that He could share our experiences in what it was like to live as a human. Not only did he live here, but he also died here for us and rose again for us. Yes, I keep saying for us. His sole purpose in coming here was to be our Savior.

Because he did these things, he made it possible for us to be made right or reconciled with God. Unless we come to believe in Jesus and what he did for us, we will still not be reconciled. It is an individual choice we all must make.

Don't delay! Make your choice to gain peace with God through the reconciliation provided by Jesus' death on the cross. Let's not be one of the enemies of God. Establish peace with him today!

Pursue the Lamb

Romans 5: 8-10

But God demonstrates his own love for us in this: While we were still sinners, Christ died for us. Since we have now been justified by his blood, how much more shall we be saved from God's wrath through him! For if, while we were God's enemies, we were reconciled to him through the death of his Son, how much more, having been reconciled, shall we be saved through his life!

Colossians 1:19-20

For God was pleased to have all his fullness dwell in him, and through him to reconcile to himself all things, whether things on earth or things in heaven, by making peace through his blood, shed on the cross.

Ephesians 2:14

For he himself is our peace, who has made the two one and has destroyed the barrier, the dividing wall of hostility.

Second Coming

2 Peter 3:15

Bear in mind that our Lord's patience means salvation, just as our dear brother Paul also wrote you with the wisdom that God gave him.

People have been talking about Jesus' second coming for over 2,000 years. I think we have become desensitized to hearing it. Mistakenly, people don't think it's ever going to happen, or at the very least, it's not going to happen during their lifetime.

But look at today's verse. The reason it's taking so long is that God has a lot of patience. He doesn't want anyone to be left out. He's being patient so more people will be saved!

Don't keep putting off your salvation thinking that you'll do it later, or that you will accept Jesus on your deathbed. What if you don't have one? What if today is the day that you go to meet Him? Or what if today is the day He comes back for His church? Please don't delay, you don't know what today will bring!

Thank God, He loves us so much! I'm glad he is patient and not in a big hurry. I still have family and friends who haven't accepted him yet. Please, Father God, be patient just a bit longer.

Pursue the Lamb

Romans 2:4

Or do you show contempt for the riches of his kindness, forbearance and patience, not realizing that God's kindness is intended to lead you to repentance?

Romans 2:7

To those who by persistence in doing good seek glory, honor and immortality, he will give eternal life.

1 Timothy 1:16

But for that very reason I was shown mercy so that in me, the worst of sinners, Christ Jesus might display his immense patience as an example for those who would believe in him and receive eternal life.

2 Peter 3:9

The Lord is not slow in keeping his promise, as some understand slowness. Instead he is patient with you, not wanting anyone to perish, but everyone to come to repentance.

The Son of God

Hebrews 1:3

The Son is the radiance of God's glory and the exact representation of his being, sustaining all things by his powerful word. After he had provided purification for sins, he sat down at the right hand of the Majesty in heaven.

I like this passage because it has several items of interest in it. I think it's because it describes Jesus our Savior. First, Jesus is the exact representation of God. He's not a knock-off. He is a perfect model because He is God. He is radiant and good and loving and kind. He's all these things because He and Father are One.

Second, Jesus sustains all things! He is our Creator, so He knows how we are made. He holds us all together as a church and He will hold you together too, when you feel like your world is falling apart.

Third, He provides purification from sin. He did that for you and me and everyone. He came to earth knowing that He was going to be the only sacrifice and the final sacrifice that would be needed.

Fourth, He is sitting, not standing at the right hand of God. He is ruling with God. He is there, watching, working, helping, comforting, loving, leading and guiding us through every day.

Does it comfort you to know that Jesus is in heaven holding all the pieces together, helping you each step of the way? It should; He's amazing!

Pursue the Lamb

John 1:14

The Word became flesh and made his dwelling among us. We have seen his glory, the glory of the one and only Son, who came from the Father, full of grace and truth.

Hebrews 7:27

Unlike the other high priests, he does not need to offer sacrifices day after day, first for his own sins, and then for sins of the people. He sacrificed for their sins once for all when he offered himself.

Titus 2:14

Who gave himself for us to redeem us from all wickedness and to purify for himself a people that are his very own, eager to do what is good.

Colossians 1:17

He is before all things, and in him all things hold together.

Run to Jesus!

Proverbs 4:12

When you walk, your steps will not be hampered; when you run, you will not stumble.

I found these three words in a devotional today! They struck a chord with me. I want to share them with you.

Run to Jesus! Run to Him. Don't walk, don't skip, don't stop in your tracks, don't strut, don't slog. RUN! I'm so thankful He is there for us to run to. Where would we be without Jesus?

He is waiting patiently for us to run to Him with everything.

Run to Him with your praise.

Run to Him with your worship.

Run to Him with thanksgiving.

Run to Him with your troubles.

Run to Him with your thoughts.

Run to Him with your sins.

Run to Him with relationships.

Run to Him with everything.

Run to Him today!

Pursue the Lamb

Proverbs 3:23

Then you will go on your way in safety, and your foot will not stumble.

Colossians 3:2

Set your minds on things above not on earthly things.

James 1:4

Let perseverance finish its work so that you may be mature and complete, not lacking anything.

James 4:7-8

Submit yourselves, then, to God. Resist the devil, and he will flee from you. Come near to God and he will come near to you.

The Bright Morning Star

Revelation 22:16

"I, Jesus, have sent my angel to give you this testimony for the churches. I am the Root and the Offspring of David, and the bright Morning Star."

Just take a few moments to list the names or perhaps actions that describe Jesus. In our verse in Revelation are just three of the many. Here are some I've come up with. I add to this list when I discover a new one.

He is:

Good, kind, love, compassionate, merciful, full of grace, a shield, protector, faithful, peaceful, omnipotent, omniscient, omnipresent, trustworthy, steadfast, the Prince of Peace, a Rock, a counselor, a dwelling place, redeemer, friend, miracle worker, way maker, powerful, and a strong tower.

I could go on and on! So can you. I challenge you today to see how many descriptive names you can find. God's Word is full of them, but there may be some that are unique to you. Give it a try, then when you are feeling down, refer back to your list and realize just how big Jesus really is. Let the list soothe your heart when you realize He's able to do and be all things.

Pursue the Lamb

Psalm 121:2

My help comes from the LORD, the Maker of heaven and earth.

Psalm 78:35

They remembered that God was their Rock, that God Most High was their Redeemer.

Judges 6:24

So Gideon built an altar to the LORD there and called it The LORD Is Peace. To this day it stands in Oprah of the Abiezrites.

Matthew 11:29

Take my yoke upon you and learn from me, for I am gentle and humble in heart, and you will find rest for your souls.

Scripture is our Bread

Matthew 4:4

Jesus answered, "It is written: 'People do not live on bread alone, but on every word that comes from the mouth of God.'"

We need a balanced diet to be a healthy person. But even that is not enough to sustain us. Eventually, our human physical bodies wear out and break down.

In the verse for today, it tells us that we need the words that come from God's mouth to sustain us. As we live for God, it becomes even more essential that we feast on the bread of His Word. What we find in His Word is our map on how to live our lives. There is advice, and direction for whatever we might encounter, there is comfort when we are hurting, assurance of His love for us when we are down.

Just as our physical bodies need food and water, so our spiritual life needs God's Spirit and His Word to sustain us. Whenever I try to diet, my husband can tell because I get "hangry". You know what I mean! It's the same way with God's Word; if we don't read it and digest it and grow from it, our spirit gets "hangry" too!

Spend time in the Word and come away satisfied. Listen to His Spirit speaking. His Word will never let us down but will keep us going every day. Don't forget to eat your daily dose of Bread.

Pursue the Lamb

Deuteronomy 8:3

He humbled you, causing you to hunger and then feeding you with manna, which neither you nor your ancestors had known, to teach you that people do not live on bread alone but on every word that comes from the mouth of the LORD.

John 4:34

"My food," said Jesus, "is to do the will of him who sent me and to finish his work."

John 6:32-33

Jesus said to them, "Very truly I tell you, it is not Moses who has given you the bread from heaven, but it is my Father who gives you the true bread from heaven. For the bread of God is the bread that comes down from heaven and gives life to the world."

Isaiah 55:2

Why spend money on what is not bread, and your labor on what does not satisfy? Listen, listen to me, and eat what is good, and you will delight in the richest of fare.

Praise the Lord, O my Soul

Psalm 103:1

Praise the LORD, my soul; all my inmost being, praise his holy name.

A song that was written using a different translation of this verse says: Bless the Lord, O my soul and all that is within me, bless His holy name.

With ALL that is within you! Can you say that? Are you praising God with ALL that is in you? I hope you are, but sometimes, in fact, a lot of times, it's hard, isn't it? Especially when you are going through a tough time. It's not always easy to praise the Lord when it seems your world is upside down.

Frankly, there are times when you just don't want to praise God. But be aware; God never goes away. He is always right there for you in the middle of that mess. He's fighting for you in ways you can't see. Yet. But you will! Don't give up. Keep trusting. Hang in there. Be still and know that He is God. You *will* be able to say, Bless the LORD, with ALL that is within me.

Pursue the Lamb

Psalm 28:6-7

Praise be to the LORD, for he has heard my cry for mercy. The Lord is my strength and my shield; my heart trusts in him, and he helps me. My heart leaps for joy, and with my song I praise him.

Psalm 104:1

Praise the LORD, my soul. LORD my God, you are very great; you are clothed with splendor and majesty.

Psalm 30:4

Sing the praises of the LORD, you his faithful people; praise his holy name.

Psalm 46:10

Be still, and know that I am God; I will be exalted among the nations. I will be exalted in the earth.

Stop Worrying

Philippians 4:6-7

Do not be anxious about anything, but in every situation, by prayer and petition, with thanksgiving, present your requests to God. And the peace of God, which transcends all understanding, will guard your hearts and your minds in Christ Jesus.

Yahweh, Jesus, Holy Spirit. As you breathe in say, "Yah," and as you breathe out say "weh". Do the same with the Name of Jesus, then the Holy Spirit. Do it again and again if you need to, until you feel yourself start to relax. Do this until you sense God's presence.

Our verse for today tells us that when we look to our Heavenly Father, He will give us His Peace. He is going to answer us. He is hearing those anxious thoughts and those fears we are voicing. Present them to God and let Him replace those burdens with His Peace.

Don't you love it that He is guarding your heart and your mind, especially when you are in the middle of a trial? Praise and thank Him today that He is smack dab in the middle of that situation you are in. Let His Peace rule today.

Pursue the Lamb

Isaiah 26:3

You will keep in perfect peace those whose minds are steadfast, because they trust in you.

Matthew 6:33-34

But seek first his kingdom and his righteousness, and all these things will be given to you as well. Therefore do not worry about tomorrow, for tomorrow will worry about itself. Each day has enough trouble of its own.

John 14:27

Peace I leave with you; my peace I give you. I do not give to you as the world gives. Do not let your hearts be troubled and do not be afraid.

Mighty Warrior

Zephaniah 3:17

The LORD your God is with you, the Mighty Warrior who saves. He will take great delight in you; in his love he will no longer rebuke you, but will rejoice over you with singing.

This verse is a tremendous promise. Take it apart piece by piece and you will see. "The LORD your God is with you the Mighty Warrior who saves." Oh my, there are many times that I need to be reassured that God is with me as a fierce protector. I'm so thankful He is my Mighty Warrior, not some puny little god made from stone or wood.

The second part says he delights in me. Sometimes I don't even delight in me, but I'm so thankful God sees me in a different light. He never stops loving me and caring about what happens to me!

The next part of the verse says, "he will no longer rebuke you, but will rejoice over you with singing. One version says, "he will quiet you with His love. I love that. God knows exactly what you need, when you need it. He will quiet you and settle you down, so you can hear the joyous song of rejoicing that He is singing over you.

Take this verse with you today, knowing that your Mighty Warrior is going with you.

Pursue the Lamb

Isaiah 63:1

Who is this coming from Edom, from Bozrah, with his garments stained crimson? Who is this, robed in splendor, striding forward in the greatness of his strength? "It is I, speaking in righteousness, mighty to save."

Exodus 15:3

The LORD is a warrior; the LORD is his name.

Ephesians 6:10

Finally, be strong in the Lord and in his mighty power.

1 Peter 5:6

Humble yourselves, therefore, under God's mighty hand, that he may lift you up in due time.

Psalm 149:4

For the LORD takes delight in his people; he crowns the humble with victory.

The Lion's Den

Daniel 6: 19-20

At the first light of dawn, the king got up and hurried to the lion's den. When he came near the den, he called to Daniel in an anguished voice, "Daniel, servant of the living God, has your God, whom you serve continually, been able to rescue you from the lions?"

In chapter six the story of Daniel in the lion's den is depicted. As I was reading along one day a couple of things stood out to me. In verse 23 it tells when Daniel was lifted out of the pit, "No wound was found on him, because he had trusted in his God."

Daniel spent the entire night with underfed lions! And yet he came out of that pit without even a tiny scratch! Do you see how amazing that is? He trusted in God to keep him safe. What are you going through that needs God's touch to keep you safe? Do you believe that you will come through this without a scratch? Trust Him; He's got this!

The second thing that stood out gives me great hope, as well. In Daniel 6:24 it says that when Daniel's enemies were thrown in with the lions, their bodies didn't even reach the floor before those same lions attacked them!

Those enemies of Daniel's and those enemies of yours will be overcome before they even have a chance to do any more damage. Put your faith and trust in God like Daniel did and come out of your situation without a scratch!

Pursue the Lamb

Daniel 6:21-22, 24

Daniel answered, "May the king live forever! My God sent his angel, and he shut the mouths of the lions. They have not hurt me, because I was found innocent in his sight. Nor have I ever done any wrong before you, Your Majesty."

24 At the kings' command, the men who had falsely accused Daniel were brought in and thrown into the lions' den, along with their wives and children. And before they reached the floor of the den, the lions overpowered them and crushed all their bones.

Isaiah 12:2

Surely God is my salvation; I will trust and not be afraid. The LORD, the LORD, is my strength and my defense; he has become my salvation.

Psalm 54:4

Surely God is my help; the LORD is the one who sustains me.

It's All Good

Romans 8:28

And we know that in all things God works for the good of those who love him, who have been called according to his purpose.

I had a friend who always said, "It's all good." It didn't seem to matter how bad things were or how stressful, it was always the same. Sometimes we wonder how anything good can come out of the situations we find ourselves in, don't we? Have you ever asked yourself that question? If you are human, you probably have asked it at some point.

We all find ourselves in hard places at times and, in the midst of those times, it is easy to get discouraged. But God has a different mindset. Thank goodness he does.

He tells us in His Word that when things happen to us who love Him that He takes all that craziness and works something beautiful out of it. He is working on changing the outcome to be the best possible answer for us! What a tremendous blessing that is for you and me.

You see, He has a purpose for us. There are things He wants us to do. No matter what is thrown at us, He will work on it and make it turn out better than we could even imagine. If we love Him and are called by Him, He *is* working on our behalf! Believe that today.

Pursue the Lamb

Genesis 50:20

You intended to harm me, but God intended it for good to accomplish what is now being done, the saving of many lives.

Jeremiah 29:11

"For I know the plans I have for you," declares the LORD, "plans to prosper you and not to harm you, plans to give you hope and a future."

Ephesians 4:14-15

Then we will no longer be infants, tossed back and forth by the waves, and blown here and there by every wind of teaching and by the cunning and craftiness of people in their deceitful scheming. Instead, speaking the truth in love, we will in all things grow up into him who is the head, that is Christ.

Put Your Armor On

Ephesians 6:11

Put on the full armor of God, so that you can take a stand against the devil's schemes.

Put on the FULL armor of God. You need every piece of the armor in order to stand firm in the battle. If you only had one piece, say, just a helmet, you would have no way to defend yourself. If you had only your sword, you could defend yourself but have no protection for your other body parts.

Without all the pieces of armor you are vulnerable. God doesn't want you to be vulnerable. He wants you to stand strong.

The pieces of armor we need are listed in Ephesians chapter 6. They are:

1. The belt of truth buckled around your waist.
2. The breastplate of righteousness
3. Shoes fit to be ready to speak the gospel of peace.
4. The shield of faith- to extinguish the flaming arrows sent your way.
5. The helmet of salvation
6. The sword of the Spirit which is the Word of God.

All these pieces are necessary to stand firm. Don't forget any of them as you get ready to face the world today. Put ALL of them on every day.

Pursue the Lamb

Romans 13:12

The night is nearly over; the day is almost here. So let us put aside the deeds of darkness and put on the armor of light.

Isaiah 11:5

Righteousness will be his belt and faithfulness the sash around his waist.

1 Thessalonians 5:8

But since we belong to the day, let us be sober, putting on faith and love as a breastplate and the hope of salvation as a helmet.

Native Language

John 8:44

You belong to your father, the devil, and you want to carry out your father's desires. He was a murderer from the beginning, not holding to the truth, for there is no truth in him. When he lies, he speaks his native language, for he is a liar and the father of lies.

I hope we know who our enemy is. I hope we know it is Satan. Jesus' words in John 8:44 tell us that he is a murderer, that there is no truth in him and he is the father of lies.

Now, since we know that, we shouldn't listen to him. He will spew bitterness and hatred into our ears, not only about others, but about ourselves too!

Don't you believe it! Instead, fill your mind with God's words. Figure out for yourself that the negative things you've been told are not true. Replace those lies with words from God himself. Scour the Bible till you find what you need to defeat the enemy. Don't let him speak his native language of lies to you any longer. Ask God to help you replace those lies with HIS truth. He is waiting to help you.

Pursue the Lamb

I John 3:8

The one who does what is sinful is of the devil, because the devil has been sinning from the beginning. The reason the Son of God appeared was to destroy the devil's work.

Genesis 3:4

"You will not certainly die," the serpent said to the woman.

Psalm 5:5-6

The arrogant cannot stand in your presence. You hate all who do wrong; you destroy those who tell lies. The bloodthirsty and the deceitful you, LORD, detest.

I John 2:22

Who is the liar? It is whoever denies that Jesus is the Messiah. Such a person is the antichrist-denying the Father and the Son.

God's Laws

Psalm 19:7

The law of the LORD is perfect, refreshing the soul. The statutes of the LORD are trustworthy, making wise the simple.

We have laws in our country for several purposes. Laws are written so we can have a peaceful place to live, and we can feel safe and secure. They are set up so that people can have a sense of orderliness. The problem though is that our laws are man-made and because of that, they are not perfect!

If you Google laws that are crazy you might find things like: Pickles should bounce, or no donkeys in bathtubs! No kidding! It's crazy that we would have laws like these on the books, but we do!

Further on in Psalm 19, we find that God's precepts (rules) are right and give us joy. His commands give us light, and His ordinances are righteous. You can see how God takes care of you when you listen to Him and follow His Word.

Thankfully, God has given us laws and statutes that are trustworthy and will make us wise. His law is perfect and given to us to keep us safe and on the right track. God loves us enough to give us rules to live by, so we can join Him someday in the mansion He's getting prepared for us. Thank You, Jesus!

Pursue the Lamb

Psalm 1:1-2

Blessed are those who do not walk in step with the wicked or stand in the way that sinners take or sit in the company of mockers, but who delight in the law of the LORD and meditate on his law day and night.

James 1:25

But those who look intently into the perfect law that gives freedom, and continue in it - not forgetting what they have heard, but doing it - they will be blessed in what they do.

Deuteronomy 4:5-6

See, I have taught you decrees and laws as the LORD my God commanded me, so that you may follow them in the land you are entering to take possession of it. Observe them carefully, for this will show your wisdom and understanding to the nations, who will hear about all these decrees and say, 'Surely this great nation is a wise and understanding people.'

Psalm 93:5

Your statutes, LORD, stand firm; holiness adorns your house for endless days.

Guard your Heart

Romans 12:2

Do not conform to the pattern of this world, but be transformed by the renewing of your mind. Then you will be able to test and approve what God's will is- his good pleasing and perfect will.

Don't be a chameleon. Chameleons tend to change their colors to match their environment. They do this so they can escape from predators. We have no need to do that because no one is trying to eat us! However, we are told in God's Word that we need to be careful about conforming to the pattern of this world. What does that mean exactly? I think it means we need to be careful not to let things into our lives that will draw us away from God. It could be anything. It will be something different for each person. You must figure out what that is for you.

Instead, we need to be transformed by the renewing of our minds. The word transformed here comes from the word, "metamorphosis", which means to change from within. God wants to change us from following the world and the mold it's trying to make us into. He wants us to be like Jesus, so He has to work on the inside. He works on our hearts, our minds, our emotions. He gives us a new way of thinking, of looking at things, and a new direction for our living.

Once we start changing from within, then we begin to see what it is He wants us to do, and we can then walk in His will. Let Him begin that process of transformation in your heart today. Walk away from the things that draw you away from His Presence. Don't let them into your heart or mind. Be transformed by the Spirit!

Pursue the Lamb

1 Peter 1:14-16

As obedient children do not conform to the evil desires you had when you lived in ignorance. But just as he who called you is holy, so be holy in all you do, for it is written: "Be holy, because I am holy."

1 John 2:15

Do not love the world or anything in the world. If you love the world, love for the Father is not in you.

2 Corinthians 10:3-4

For though we live in the world, we do not wage war as the world does. The weapons we fight with are not the weapons of the world. On the contrary, they have divine power to demolish strongholds.

Rely on God's Strength

Zechariah 4:6

So he said to me, "This is the word of the LORD to Zerubbabel: 'Not by might nor by power, but by my Spirit,' says the LORD Almighty.'"

Sometimes in life we encounter things that are very difficult. It may seem that there is no good solution. Beating your head against a brick wall will give you nothing but a headache.

I'm so glad that God's word tells us that the only place there is might and power is in the Holy Spirit. Anything we try to do will only cause hurt feelings, or failure.

Let God have that difficult thing and then stand back and watch! It's going to be good, because he promises in Romans 8:28: "We know that in ALL things God works for the good of those who love him, who have been called according to his purpose.

It's not might or power or anything else we do that will bring us peace; it's God's Spirit.

Pursue the Lamb

2 Chronicles 20:15-17

He said: "Listen King Jehoshaphat and all who live in Judah and Jerusalem! This is what the LORD says to you: 'Do not be afraid or discouraged because of this vast army. For the battle is not yours, but God's. Tomorrow march down against them. They will be climbing up by the Pass of Ziz and you will find them at the end of the gorge in the Desert of Jeruel. You will not have to fight this battle. Take up your positions, stand firm and see the deliverance the LORD will give you, Judah and Jerusalem. Do not be afraid; do not be discouraged. Go out to face them tomorrow and the LORD will be with you.

Philippians 2:12-13

Therefore, my dear friends, as you have always obeyed - not only in my presence, but now much more in my absence – continue to work out your salvation with fear and trembling, for it is God who works in you to will and to act in order to fulfill his good purpose.

Romans 8:9

You, however, are not controlled by the sinful nature but are in the Spirit, if indeed the Spirit of God lives in you. And if anyone does not have the Spirit of Christ, they do not belong to Christ.

Turn Around

Acts 3:19

Repent, then, and turn to God, so that your sins may be wiped out, that times of refreshing may come from the Lord.

Repent, turn, convert... all three of these words mean basically the same thing! When you repent, you tell God that you are sorry for the wrong things you've done in your life, then you start living the way He wants you to live. Kind of like a U turn.

If you are asking Him to forgive you, that means that you want to turn away from those things and start doing what is right!

Convert also means to "turn" away from doing something. If we are really serious about the Good News of Jesus, we should want to turn from those things that would lead us the wrong way.

The last part of the verse for today tells us that when we do these things, that times of refreshing will come from the LORD. He will give you joy and peace and your soul will find rest. Hallelujah!

Please help us, Jesus, to follow Your lead and repent, turn and convert. Help us make a 180-degree turn, so we can be at peace with You!

Pursue the Lamb

Jeremiah 6:16

This is what the LORD says: "Stand at the crossroads and look; ask for the ancient paths, ask where the good way is, and walk in it, and you will find rest for your souls. But you said, "We will not walk in it."

1 Kings 8:58

May he turn our hearts to him, to walk in obedience to him and keep the commands, decrees and laws he gave our ancestors.

Isaiah 1:18-19

"Come now, let us reason together," says the LORD. "Though your sins are like scarlet, they shall be as white as snow; though they are red as crimson, they shall be like wool. If you are willing and obedient, you will eat the best from the land."

Instruct the Wise

Proverbs 9:9

"Instruct the wise and they will be wiser still; teach the righteous and they will add to their learning."

This verse speaks to my teacher heart. I love it when God gives me a verse in His Word that helps me out and gives me peace amid my chaos.

This verse was given to me the same day I had a speaking engagement at a women's retreat. I was nervous to say the least, but God, He knows all about me and He knows what I needed to hear that day. He was telling me that I was getting ready to teach these ladies something He had for them. Something that was going to help them grow and become wiser. I love that!

God wants you to be wise.

God will give you words to live by too, if you get in His Word, His book, and let His Holy Spirit open your heart and mind. You'll be amazed at the things He will teach you. Then maybe you can pass that on to someone else, and add to their learning.

Pursue the Lamb

Proverbs 1:5, 7

5 Let the wise listen and add to their learning, and let the discerning get guidance...

7 The fear of the LORD is the beginning of knowledge, but fools despise wisdom and instruction.

Proverbs 14:6

The mocker seeks wisdom and finds none, but knowledge comes easily to the discerning.

Titus 2:1

You, however, must teach what is appropriate to sound doctrine.

Titus 2:12-15

It teaches us to say "NO" to ungodliness and worldly passions, and to live self-controlled, upright and godly lives in this present age, while we wait for the blessed hope-the appearing of the glory of our great God and Savior, Jesus Christ, who gave himself for us to redeem us from all wickedness and purify for himself a people that are his very own, eager to do what is good. These then are the things you should teach. Encourage and rebuke with all authority. Do not let anyone despise you.

Ask God

James 1:5-6 NIV

If you want to know what God wants you to do, ask him and he will gladly tell you, for he is always ready to give a bountiful supply of wisdom to all who ask him; he will not resent it. But when you ask him, be sure that you really expect him to tell you, for a doubtful mind will be as unsettled as a wave of the sea that is driven and tossed by the wind.

I've never spent much time around the ocean, but enough to know that I wouldn't want to be on a boat being tossed around by the waves! It would not be a good feeling to have the floor drop out from under you, or your shoulder plastered into a wall as the boat takes a dip.

However, isn't this how we feel sometimes when we are in the process of trying to make decisions? I find myself trying to make up my mind and at times floundering around horribly.

Our verses today tell us that if we really want to know what we should do, we need to ask God, with the faith that He *will* give us the answer, and He will gladly tell us. He has a supply of wisdom far beyond anything we are capable of dreaming up.

Ephesians 3:20 says: Now to him who is able to do *immeasurably* more than all we ask or imagine according to his power that is at work in us"… *Immeasurably more.* Did you catch that phrase? It means that we can't even begin to imagine how God is going to fix that problem that is on our hearts, but He will. He has a plan. Do we trust him enough to let Him take care of it for us?

Don't let that raging sea get the better of you. Trust God for the answers today.

Pursue the Lamb

Matthew 21:22

"If you believe, you will receive whatever you ask for in prayer."

Mark 11:24

"Therefore I tell you, whatever you ask for in prayer, believe that you have received it, and it will be yours."

Proverbs 2:3-6

Indeed, if you call out for insight and cry aloud for understanding, and if you look for it as for silver and search for it as for hidden treasure, then you will understand the fear of the LORD and find the knowledge of God. For the LORD gives wisdom; from his mouth come knowledge and understanding.

Our Seeking God

Ezekiel 34:11-12

For this is what the Sovereign LORD says: I myself will search for my sheep and look after them. As a shepherd looks after his scattered flock when he is with them, so will I look after my sheep. I will rescue them from all the places where they were scattered on a day of clouds and darkness.

The Israelites must have felt lost. Jerusalem was gone, burned to the ground. Their priests and kings were no longer leading like they should. The people were scattered all over the land. What an awful feeling to know that life as they knew it, would never be the same.

Have you been there? Has something major happened in your life that causes such an upheaval that you are not sure how to carry on?

There is good news! Our verses today say that God himself will search for you and look after you. He *will* find you. He will find your son or daughter, or your grandchildren. He will step into your situation and continue to work. Yes, I said continue, because He's always been there even during the clouds and darkness, working, working, working for the situation to have the very best outcome possible.

You can be certain that He is looking after you and yours. What a peace we can have to know that Our Shepherd will not leave us alone on the hillside. He will ALWAYS come looking for us.

Pursue the Lamb

Psalm 119:176

I have strayed like a lost sheep. Seek your servant, for I have not forgotten your commands.

Isaiah 40:11

He tends his flock like a shepherd: He gathers the lambs in his arms and carries them close to his heart; he gently leads those that have young.

Jeremiah 31:10

Hear the word of the LORD, you nations; proclaim it in the distant coastlands: He who scattered Israel will gather them and will watch over his flock like a shepherd.

Luke 19:10

"For the Son of Man came to seek and to save what was lost."

God's Plans for You

Jeremiah 29:11

For I know the plans I have for you," declares the LORD, "plans to prosper you and not to harm you, plans to give you hope and a future."

What a wonderful promise from God! He knows what is going to happen and it's going to be good! You can trust Him when He says that. His plan is to prosper you and not to harm you. That doesn't necessarily mean that He's going to make you rich. There are many ways in which God can prosper you. If you can't believe that, at least know that He is not out to harm you. He loves you too much for that!

You may be going through a rough time right now and the future may look bleak, but if you really seek God, (keep reading the next few verses Jeremiah 29:12-14), and search for Him with all your heart, you will find Him.

His promise to you is that He will give you hope. That little spark of hope is sometimes all you need to fan your faith into flame. Keep searching, praying, listening, working diligently. Your future is in the hands of the Master. He knows the plans. Trust His heart.

Pursue the Lamb

Jeremiah 29:12-14

"Then you will call on me and come and pray to me, and I will listen to you. You will seek me and find me when you seek me with all your heart. I will be found by you," declares the LORD, "and will bring you back from captivity. I will gather you from all the nations and places where I have banished you," declares the LORD, "and will bring you back to the place from which I carried you into exile."

Psalm 40:5

Many, LORD my God, are the wonders you have done, the things you planned for us. None can compare with you; were I to speak and tell of your deeds, they would be too many to declare.

Isaiah 55:9

"As the heavens are higher than the earth, so are my ways higher than your ways and my thoughts than your thoughts."

Lie Down and Rest

Ezekiel 34:15 and Psalm 23:1-2

"I myself will tend my sheep and have them lie down", declares the Sovereign LORD.

Psalm 23:1-2

The LORD is my Shepherd, I lack nothing. He makes me lie down in green pastures, he leads me beside quiet waters.

When I am tired, I just want to lie down. I want to rest and not have to think about much of anything. Our verses today tell us that we have a Shepherd who will let us rest. He doesn't keep driving us on. He gives you and I food, shelter, and rest.

You don't have to be afraid because you know the One who is taking care of you. He knows when you are tired. He knows that the load you are carrying is heavy. He sees that situation you are in at work. When things are not going well in your marriage or with your kids, He sees that too!

He tells us in His Word that He will make you lie down and give you rest and peace. Let Him. Let Him speak words of peace and comfort to your soul. Meditate on His Word. Listen carefully to His instructions. Trust Him to lead you by still water. Let Him restore your soul. Lie still and hear Him today!

Pursue the Lamb

Isaiah 40:11

He tends his flock like a shepherd; He gathers the lambs in his arms and carries them close to his heart; he gently leads those that have young.

Micah 5:4

He will stand and shepherd his flock in the strength of the LORD, in the majesty of the name of the LORD his God. And they will live securely, for then his greatness will reach to the ends of the earth.

Psalm 23:3-4

He refreshes my soul. He guides me along the right paths for his name's sake. Even though I walk through the darkest valley, I will fear no evil, for you are with me; your rod and your staff, they comfort me.

The Voice of God

Read Psalm 29 on the facing page.

Psalm 29 is full of vivid mental pictures of what the voice of God is like. Just listen to some of the descriptions given.

His Voice thunders, it is powerful, majestic, it breaks cedars, it can strike like lightening, it twists oaks! And the list goes on. Wow!

Those are all amazing things. As a matter of fact, these things were symbols of strength to the ancient peoples. They are to us today, too! God is mighty and powerful and amazing. Spend a moment thinking about the descriptions of God's voice.

But verse eleven is the one that grabs my attention the most. "The LORD gives strength to his people; the LORD blesses his people with peace. What amazes me is that the same God who thunders and is powerful and can strike like lightening cares enough about ME that He gives me strength and peace to get through this life. Listen for Him today. You might hear Him in thunder or a hurricane, but most likely you'll hear a still small voice. Embrace His Voice today. Let Him give you His Peace.

Pursue the Lamb

Psalm 29

Ascribe to the LORD, you heavenly beings, ascribe to the LORD glory and strength.

Ascribe to the LORD the glory due his name; worship the LORD in the splendor of his holiness.

The voice of the LORD is over the waters; the God of glory thunders, the LORD thunders over the mighty waters.

The voice of the LORD is powerful; the voice of the LORD is majestic.

The voice of the LORD breaks the cedars; the LORD breaks in pieces the cedars of Lebanon.

He makes Lebanon leap like a calf, Sirion like a young wild ox.

The voice of the LORD strikes with flashes of lightning.

The voice of the LORD shakes the desert; the LORD shakes the Desert of Kadesh.

The voice of the LORD twists the oaks and strips the forests bare.

And in his temple all cry, "Glory!"

The LORD sits enthroned over the flood; the LORD is enthroned as King forever.

The LORD gives strength to his people; the LORD blesses his people with peace.

The Light Shines On

John 1:5 AMP

"The Light shines on in the darkness and the darkness did not understand it or overpower it or appropriate it or absorb it (and is unreceptive to it)."

The Light with a capital L. Did you notice that capital? Jesus is that Light! He's the One who came to bring us out of the darkness of sin and give us new life!

But look at the rest of that verse. When He came, we didn't understand Him. Why would He leave heaven and come here to earth to die for us? One simple word. Love! He loved us that much!

The rest of the verse says Jesus was never overpowered. He was never at a loss; He went willingly to the cross. He wasn't appropriated, meaning He wasn't used without His permission. He left heaven of His own accord.

He wasn't absorbed or taken in by the darkness either. He remained the True Light, shining even in the worst hours of His life and yours too!

The saddest part of the verse is in the parentheses. Some of us are unreceptive to His Light. The darkness can seem overpowering; it makes us confused and tries to absorb us. But the Good News is that Jesus has already defeated that darkness. Give Him a chance today. Turn to the Light with a capital L.

Pursue the Lamb

John 1:4

In him was life, and that life was the light of all people.

John 8:12

When Jesus spoke again to the people, he said, "I am the light of the world. Whoever follows me will never walk in darkness, but will have the light of life."

Ephesians 5:8-10

For you were once darkness, but now you are light in the Lord. Live as children of light (for the fruit of the light consists in all goodness, righteousness and truth) and find out what pleases the Lord.

1 Thessalonians 5:5

You are all children of the light and children of the day. We do not belong to the night or to the darkness.

Silver and Gold

Proverbs 27:21

The crucible for silver and the furnace for gold, but people are tested by their praise.

A crucible is used to melt down silver and a furnace melts gold. Both elements are being subjected to high heat. The heat is changing their property of being a solid into being a liquid. This heat is testing for any impurities in the metals.

The second part of the verse says that people, instead of being put to the fire, are tested by the praise they receive. In other words, do we become proud or puffed up when people compliment us? How many times have we allowed flattery to make us think highly of ourselves? Another way of saying it is, we are tested for impurities in our thinking, too, by the praise of people.

Just like the gold and silver melt at high temperatures, we can find ourselves melting over praise. Always be careful to give praise to the One who really deserves it.

Pursue the Lamb

I Chronicles 29:17

I know my God, that you test the heart and are pleased with integrity. All these things have I given willingly and with honest intent. And now I have seen with joy how willingly your people who are here have given to you.

Psalm 26:2

Test me, LORD, and try me, examine my heart and my mind.

Psalm 139:23-24

Search me, God, and know my heart; test me and know my anxious thoughts. See if there is any offensive way in me, and lead me in the way everlasting.

I Peter 1:7

These have come so that your faith - of greater worth than gold, which perishes even though refined by fire - may be proved genuine and may result in praise, glory and honor when Jesus Christ is revealed.

Hemmed In

Psalm 139:5

You hem me in behind and before, and you lay your hand upon me.

God is omniscient or all knowing. He knows all about you. He knows your likes, and your dislikes and yet He loves you. It doesn't matter where you go, what you do, who you talk to, or what you eat, He still loves you with an everlasting love.

He goes before you, and He is your rear-facing guard as well. He has you hemmed in, similar to when you are stuck in a traffic jam. You can't go forward or backward without Him being there.

Just rest easy knowing He has control of the flow of traffic in your life. Doesn't that give you comfort and peace, knowing that He is surrounding you, keeping you safe? He knows your past and He knows your future. If you were to go to the left or the right, He would still be there. He has His hand on you.

When it's time to move, you will know. You will sense His hand upon your life knowing He has your future under control.

Pursue the Lamb

Psalm 32:10

Many are the woes of the wicked, but the LORD's unfailing love surrounds those who trust in him.

Psalm 34:7

The angel of the LORD encamps around those who fear him, and he delivers them.

Psalm 125:2

As the mountains surround Jerusalem, so the LORD surrounds his people both now and forevermore.

Forget not all His Benefits

Psalms 103:2-3

Praise the LORD, my soul and forget not all his benefits, who forgives all your sins, and heals all your diseases.

What has God done for you or given you lately? Grab a piece of paper or use a journal and make a list. Oh, my goodness! The things He has done should amaze you! Don't forget those benefits of love, grace, mercy and all the material things He has given you. Those are icing on the cake, so to speak.

The first part of verse three says, He forgives all your sins. If that were the only thing he ever did for you, you would be more than favored.

Praise the Lord for forgiving you for your sins. Think about what it cost Jesus to do this for you. If He hadn't been willing to go to the cross and die and rise again, you would still be lost in your sin and headed for a place called Hell.

Even if He never gave you one more thing, having your sins removed and being made free would be enough! I'm glad He doesn't stop there though, He helps you through every single day, loving you and giving you the strength to go on.

I'm so thankful for Jesus! He is worth praising. Oh, and don't forget all His benefits!

Pursue the Lamb

Psalm 106:1

Give thanks to the LORD, for he is good; his love endures forever.

Psalm 117

Praise the LORD, all you nations;

extol him, all you peoples.

For great is his love toward us,

and the faithfulness of the LORD endures forever.

Praise the LORD.

Psalm 77:11

I will remember the deeds of the LORD; yes, I will remember your miracles of long ago.

1 Peter 2:24

He himself bore our sins in his body on the cross, so that we might die to sins and live for righteousness; by his wounds you have been healed.

The Image of the Invisible God

Colossians 1:15-20

The Son is the image of the invisible God, the firstborn over all creation. For in him all things were created: things in heaven and on earth, visible and invisible, whether thrones or powers or rulers or authorities; all things have been created through him and for him. He is before all things, and in him all things hold together. And he is the head of the body, the church; he is the beginning and the firstborn from among the dead, so that in everything he might have the supremacy. For God was pleased to have all his fullness dwell in him, and through him to reconcile to himself all things, whether things on earth or things in heaven, by making peace through his blood shed on the cross.

Sometimes, when I read a long passage like this, I find that I must break it down into a more readable format for my brain to understand what is being said. As I read this passage and checked commentaries for meaning, I found that if I put it in prayer form, it made perfect sense. So here goes:

> Jesus, You the Son, are the image of the invisible God, the firstborn over all creation. In You all things were created; things in heaven and on earth, visible and invisible, whether thrones, or powers or rulers or authorities; all things have been created through You and for You. You, Jesus, are before all things, and in You all things hold together. (You are the cement!) And You

are the head of the body, the church; You are the beginning and the firstborn from among the dead, so that in everything You might have the supremacy. For God was pleased to have all His fullness dwell in You, and through You to reconcile to Himself all things, whether things on earth or things in heaven, by making peace through Your blood, shed on the cross.

Jesus is what holds us together as a person and as a church. He is the glue. He is our Savior. Hallelujah!

Pursue the Lamb

John 1:18
No one has ever seen God, but the one and only Son, who is himself God and is in closest relationship with the Father, has made him known.

Philippians 2:9-10
Therefore God exalted him to the highest place and gave him the name that is above every name, that at the name of Jesus every knee should bow, in heaven and on earth and under the earth.

Crowns with Love and Compassion

Psalm 103:4

Who redeems your life from the pit and crowns you with love and compassion.

The notes in my study Bible says the "pit" is a metaphor for the grave, and "redeems" is a synonym for delivers. Basically, the first part of verse four is saying, Jesus delivers us from death! How does He accomplish this deliverance from death? It's already been done through His life and death and resurrection! You have been given a gift that you need to cherish.

Not only does He deliver you from death, meaning you will go to be with Him when you die, but He gives you grace to live for Him until He returns. Then He gives you love and mercy so you can help other people see how much He loves them. You are given love for others and can be compassionate because God gives you those abilities.

So, two things from today's verse. Thank God for having a plan to rescue you from death. Second, think about who needs to see God through your love and mercy today.

Pursue the Lamb

Psalm 56:13

For you have delivered me from death and my feet from stumbling, that I may walk before God in the light of life.

Isaiah 43:1

But now, this is what the LORD says- he who created you, Jacob, he who formed you, Israel: "Do not fear, for I have redeemed you; I have summoned you by name; you are mine."

Psalm 34:22

The LORD redeems his servants; no one who takes refuge in him will be condemned.

Hosea 13:14

"I will deliver them from the power of the grave; I will redeem them from death. Where, O death, are your plagues? Where, O grave, is your destruction?

I AM, on the Path

Psalm 16:11

You make known to me the path of life; you will fill me with joy in your presence, with eternal pleasures at your right hand.

Jesus said in John 14:6, "I am the way, the truth and the life." He is our path. If we follow Him and go where He leads us we can't go wrong. Our verse today says He will fill us with joy and eternal pleasures.

Will following Jesus always be easy? Don't believe for one moment that this path of Christianity will be a cake walk! This path will have you trudging up hills and possibly a mountainside, or you may be picking your way down into a valley.

Whichever situation you find yourself in, please know that Jesus is right there with you. Let God fill you with joy by spending time in His presence. Look to Him to light your path and trust that He knows all the curves and hills. He also knows what is at the end of that path and has things all worked out just for you!

Stay on the path with the Great I AM! It is worth it in the end, and you will see those eternal pleasures come to pass.

Pursue the Lamb

Psalm 139:23-24

Search me, God, and know my heart; test me and know my anxious thoughts. See if there is any offensive way in me, and lead me in the way everlasting.

Matthew 7:13-14

"Enter through the narrow gate. For wide is the gate and broad is the road that leads to destruction, and many enter through it. But small is the gate and narrow the road that leads to life, and only a few find it.

Acts 2:28

You have made known to me the path of life; you will fill me with joy in your presence.

His Love Endures Forever

Psalm 136:1-3

Give thanks to the LORD, for he is good. His love endures forever. Give thanks to the God of gods. His love endures forever. Give thanks to the LORD of lords: His love endures forever.

If you've read the Psalms, you know the phrase: His love endures forever. It shows up 26 times in Psalm 136, but it is also in other places in the Bible as well. Just stop what you are doing and think about what that verse really means.

The word, love, or "hesed" in Hebrew, has a variety of meanings. It is an attempt in our English language to say that God is compassionate and kind, that He loves you, has mercy on you. According to our Bible verses with this phrase, this love goes on and on forever and ever. Endures means it will remain in existence forever!

Isn't it great to know that God will always be there, loving you? We should want to serve Him because He never stops loving us. No matter what!

Pursue the Lamb

Psalm 136:26

Give thanks to the God of heaven. His love endures forever.

Psalm 105:1

Give praise to the LORD, call on his name; make known among the nations what he has done.

Deuteronomy 10:17

For the LORD your God is God of gods and Lord of lords, the great God, mighty and awesome, who shows no partiality and accepts no bribes.

The Seven-Fold Spirit of God

Revelation 5:6

Then I saw a Lamb looking as if it had been slain, standing in the center before the throne, encircled by the four living creatures and the elders. The Lamb had seven horns and seven eyes, which are the seven spirits of God sent out into all the earth.

The books of Revelation and Isaiah both mention the seven-fold Spirit of God. As you probably know, seven is a number used repeatedly in the Bible. It denotes completeness.

The Revelation passage and Isaiah 11:1-2 both speak of Jesus or the Branch, also named the Lamb. The seven Spirits are found in the Holy Spirit. He is the first overall Spirit, then in him are the other six.

When Isaiah was prophesying about the Messiah, he was telling us that Jesus would be complete because He would have the Holy Spirit of God rest upon Him. Then He would be empowered to carry out the other six purposes of God. According to Isaiah, Jesus would have the Spirit of wisdom, the Spirit of understanding, the Spirit of counsel, the Spirit of might, the Spirit of the knowledge and the Spirit of the fear of the LORD.

Jesus is complete. Nothing needs to be added. He is perfection because He is God, He is the Son of God and He is the Holy Spirit.

Pursue the Lamb

John 1:29

The next day John saw Jesus coming toward him and said, "Look the Lamb of God, who takes away the sin of the world!"

Isaiah 11:1-2

A shoot will come up from the stump of Jesse; from his roots a Branch will bear fruit. The Spirit of the LORD will rest on him – the Spirit of wisdom and of understanding, the Spirit of counsel and of might, the Spirit of the knowledge and fear of the LORD…

Revelation 1:4-5

John,

To the seven churches in the province of Asia: Grace and peace to you from him who is, and who was, and who is to come, and from the seven spirits before his throne and from Jesus Christ, who is the faithful witness, the firstborn from the dead, and the ruler of the kings of the earth.

Watch Where You're Walking, Standing and Sitting

Psalm 1:1

Blessed are those who do not walk in step with the wicked or stand in the way that sinners take or sit in the company of mockers.

Did you read that verse? I mean really read it. If you did, I hope you saw what I saw. Three things popped out at me: We shouldn't walk, stand or sit with evil.

What does that look like in your life? It pretty much covers all our life while we are awake, doesn't it? When you're walking, be careful where you go. When you're standing, be aware of who is around you. When you're sitting down, be careful who you're talking to and what you are seeing.

The next verse says if you are obedient while walking, standing and sitting and delight in God's Word and study it, you will be blessed. Be aware of what is going on around you. It was important enough that God had it put in His Word. There must be a reason, don't you think?

Pursue the Lamb

Psalm 89:15

Blessed are those who have learned to acclaim you, who walk in the light of your presence, LORD.

Proverbs 1:8-9

Listen, my son, to your father's instruction and do not forsake your mother's teaching. They are a garland to grace your head and a chain to adorn your neck.

Proverbs 4:26-27

Give careful thought to the paths for your feet and be steadfast in all your ways. Do not turn to the right or the left; keep your foot from evil.

Cleansed from Sin

I John 1:7

But if we walk in the light as he is in the light, we have fellowship with one another, and the blood of Jesus, his Son, cleanses us from all sin.

If you read that verse closely you might have picked up on two things. First, IF we are walking in the Light, we will have good relationships with other people. It says we have fellowship with one another. Fellowship means we are friendly with other people who have a common interest! Isn't that what we enjoy with fellow Christians? We definitely have a common interest in Jesus. We should be treating each other with genuine respect and love.

The second thing found in that verse says that Jesus' blood cleanses us. Notice that the word "cleanses" is present tense, not past tense. This cleansing is ongoing in our Christian walk. As we live our lives, there will be times we mess up and do things we shouldn't. But then there is Jesus. He's looking at you and saying, "I can clean that up for you." That is His sustaining grace at work. Jesus is always there, keeping you on the right path, walking alongside you, helping you, cleansing you, sustaining you every step of the way home. We only have to ask for His help.

Pursue the Lamb

Hebrews 9:14

How much more, then, will the blood of Christ, who through the eternal Spirit offered himself unblemished to God, cleanse our consciences from acts that lead to death, so that we may serve the living God!

Revelation 7:14

I answered, "Sir you know." And he said, "These are they who have come out of the great tribulation; they have washed their robes and made them white in the blood of the Lamb."

Isaiah 2:5

Come, house of Jacob, let us walk in the light of the LORD.

Called for a Purpose

1 Corinthians 10:31

So, whether you eat or drink or whatever you do, do it all for the glory of God.

"Seek to be the person God has called you to be." This was a quote from Dr. Charles Stanley in the In Touch magazine. It caught my attention. Who has God equipped you to be? Has He equipped you to teach or preach? Maybe, but what if He equipped you to be say, a chef? Or a firefighter? Or a pilot?

Does it really matter what skills He's given you as long as you use them to bring honor and glory to Him?

That is the key isn't it? Whatever God has asked of us, He has also equipped us for! We need to SEEK to be THAT person. You know, the stay-at-home mom, raising little ones. How about the person in the cubicle at the office or the clerk at the grocery store? It doesn't matter, you know, where you are in life, or what your skill set may be. Seek after God, honor Him with your life. Bring glory to Him! He's had a plan for you all along.

Pursue the Lamb

Colossians 3:17

And whatever you do, whether in word or deed, do it all in the name of the Lord Jesus, giving thanks to God the Father through Him.

1 Peter 4:11

If you speak, you should do so as one who speaks the very words of God. If you serve, you should do so with the strength God provides, so that in all things God may be praised through Jesus Christ. To him be the glory and the power for ever and ever. Amen.

Romans 11:36

For from Him and through Him and to Him are all things. To Him be the glory forever! Amen.

Be a Sheep

John 10:27 Amp

The sheep that are My own hear My voice and listen to me; I know them, and they follow me.

I've been told by those who know me and who've heard me speak or teach, that they hear my voice when they read my books. Because they know me, and the sound of my voice, it helps them understand my words and nuances. I hope they are learning and listening to the things I'm telling them about Jesus most of all!

Here is the awesome thing about today's verse in John chapter ten. Jesus is saying that if we are His, we will recognize His Voice. According to the verse, if we know Him and follow Him because He is the author, the source of the Words, then we will know Who is speaking to us. In the first chapter of John, he says, "In the beginning was the word." That WORD is Jesus.

If we know Him, we will follow Him because He's given us a master plan, the Bible, and we will be able to hear and understand Him when He is speaking to us. Give it a try. Listen for His Voice today while you are reading His Word.

Pursue the Lamb

John 10:4

When he has brought out all his own, he goes on ahead of them, and his sheep follow him because they know his voice.

Psalm 50:14-15

Sacrifice thank offerings to God, fulfill your vows to the Most High, and call on me in the day of trouble; I will deliver you, and you will honor me.

Psalm 46:10

Be still and know that I am God; I will be exalted among the nations, I will be exalted in the earth.

Consider it Pure Joy

James 1:2-3

Consider it pure joy, my brothers and sisters, whenever you face trials of many kinds, because you know that the testing of your faith produces perseverance.

What do you do when you consider something? What does that word really mean anyway? Check out just about any dictionary definition of the word "consider" and here is what you will see; "to think about seriously; to regard as; to believe after deliberation."

If you apply this definition to the verse above, here is a possible meaning. We are to think hard about the trials and things that come into our lives. Not only are we to think hard about it, but we are supposed to be joyful about it, too! Wow! That is a hard thing to do sometimes, isn't it? Why would James tell us to be joyful about a situation that is beyond our control?

I believe the answer lies with Jesus! We need to stop, slow down and think about what is going on in a calm manner. We must let Jesus come to us and help us see that He is in control and working in our situation. Ask Him to help you see what is going on through His eyes. He will give you the perseverance (see verse 3) to go on, no matter how long it may take.

We only develop perseverance when there are hard times. However, we are to look at these hard times with joy and learn and grow from them. If you are going through a difficult time right now, give it to Jesus! He can handle it.

Pursue the Lamb

Matthew 5:12

Rejoice and be glad, because great is your reward in heaven, for in the same way they persecuted the prophets who were before you.

Hebrews 10:35-36

So do not throw away your confidence; it will be richly rewarded. You need to persevere so that when you have done the will of God, you will receive what he has promised.

1 Peter 1:7

These have come so that your faith-of greater worth than gold, which perishes even though refined by fire-may be proved genuine and may result in praise, glory and honor when Jesus Christ is revealed.

Be Content

Psalm 131:2

But I have calmed and quieted myself. I am like a weaned child with its mother, like a weaned child I am content.

When a calf is taken from its mother it is not a happy camper. If you've ever been around when this happens, you understand someone is not in love with what's happening!

Young children have some similar reactions when they are being weaned. They might cry or be fussy more and they, like the calves, will be more vocal. But our verse today tells of a child that has learned to calm itself down and be content.

How do we do this? How can we calm ourselves before God? We must set aside time to get alone with Him. Just be...

Be quiet.

Be listening.

Be waiting.

When we do this, when we wait to hear from God, He will not disappoint. Be like that child who has learned to be content. Do you feel yourself calming down? Rest and wait.

Pursue the Lamb

Psalm 116:7

Return to your rest, my soul, for the LORD has been good to you.

Psalm 91:1

Whoever dwells in the shelter of the Most High will rest in the shadow of the Almighty.

Psalm 90:14

Satisfy us in the morning with your unfailing love, that we may sing for joy and be glad all our days.

Guilty Conscience

Psalm 32:5

Then I acknowledged my sin to you and did not cover up my iniquity. I said, "I will confess by transgressions to the LORD." And you forgave the guilt of my sin.

When I was a little girl, I had a conscience that worked overtime. It seemed I was always feeling guilty about something I had done. Once I told my mom about it, the guilt would go away. I was young enough that I didn't know I could go to Jesus and let Him take care of it.

Our verse today tells us we shouldn't try to cover up the things that we know are wrong. The Psalmist David must have dealt with a guilty conscience, too! He made it a point to confess his sins to God. Only then could he be free from the guilt.

You know, it's the same way for us today. Tell the Lord what you've done. Ask for forgiveness and let Him lift that load of guilt so you can be free!

Pursue the Lamb

Proverbs 28:13

Those who conceal their sins do not prosper, but those who confess and renounce them find mercy.

1 John 1:9

If we confess our sins, he is faithful and just and will forgive us our sins and purify us from all unrighteousness.

Micah 7:18

Who is a God like you, who pardons sin and forgives the transgression of the remnant of his inheritance? You do not stay angry forever but delight to show mercy.

Solid Food

Hebrews 5:14

But solid food is for the mature, who by constant use have trained themselves to distinguish good from evil.

Think about toddlers. It sometimes seems like they are into everything! You might find yourself plugging the electrical outlets, baby proofing your cabinets, etc. You get the picture. The reason for all this caution is because little children can't discern what is good for them and what is bad. They don't have the knowledge yet because they have not matured. They need to learn a lot of new things as they are growing into better understanding.

We, too, have to grow in our faith in a very similar way. We must train ourselves to see the difference between good and evil. Will we be perfect at it right away? Of course not! Just like a child learning not to touch something hot, we can learn through our experiences what we should and shouldn't do. If we stay in God's word and do what it says, we should become more and more mature. It won't lead us down the wrong path.

Once we have learned that something is wrong and not what we should be doing, we must ask forgiveness and then move on and not do it again. God is always ready to forgive us and help us do what is right.

I believe God shields us from some things, like we do for our toddlers, until we learn to do better and become more mature. Let's strive to grow up in the Word and eat solid food.

Pursue the Lamb

Ephesians 4:15

Instead, speaking the truth in love, we will in all things grow up into him who is the head, that is, Christ.

John 4:34

"My food," said Jesus, "is to do the will of him who sent me to finish his work."

Deuteronomy 8:3

He humbled you, causing you to hunger and then feeding you with manna, which neither you nor your ancestors had known, to teach you that people do not live on bread alone but on every word that comes from the mouth of the LORD.

Rainbow Promises

Gen 9: 8, 13

[8]Then God said to Noah and to his sons with him: I will establish my covenant with you and with your descendants after you…

[13]I have set my rainbow in the clouds, and it will be the sign of the covenant between me and the earth.

It was 2004. It was a crazy, sad year in my world. In May of that year, our 20-year-old daughter was killed in a car accident. You can imagine our devastation. We went around in shock for quite a long time, but about a week after the accident, my younger daughter was graduating from high school. So, yes, I buried a child and a week later sat and watched one graduate.

At the end of that same summer, I had to watch my graduate go off to college for the first time. Here is where the rainbow of God's promise to me comes into effect.

On our way to drop off our daughter and get her moved into the dorm, we saw a beautiful rainbow. I didn't think too much about it at the time, but as my husband and I drove back home without our girl, there it was! Another rainbow!

It was as if God was saying to me, "I promise with the first rainbow that I'm taking care of daughter number one. With the second rainbow, I'm taking care of daughter number two." What a great promise for this mama's heart that was emotional for so many reasons. Both girls were going to be OK.

But God wasn't done yet! Fast forward four years. At the after-graduation party for daughter number two, guess what appeared in the sky? Yes! Another rainbow, capping both ends of those college years, with promises of His love and care! Isn't God amazing!!!!

Pursue the Lamb

Isaiah 54:10-11

As the rain and the snow come down from heaven, and do not return to it without watering the earth, and making it bud and flourish, so that it yields seed for the sower and bread for the eater, so is my word that goes out from my mouth; it will not return to me empty, but will accomplish what I desire and achieve the purpose for which I sent it.

Revelation 4:3

And the one who sat there had the appearance of jasper and ruby. A rainbow that shone like an emerald encircled the throne.

Psalm 145:13

Your kingdom is an everlasting kingdom, and your dominion endures through all generations. The LORD is trustworthy in all he promises and faithful in all he does.

Kindness and Compassion

Ephesians 4:32

Be kind and compassionate to one another forgiving each other, just as in Christ God forgave you.

We sure have been hearing a lot about being kind lately. But guess what? The Bible has been telling us this for years! This concept is not new!

There is a lot packed into this verse. Being kind is one, but being compassionate is another. When we are compassionate, we have sympathy for someone who is in a bad place. Does that sound like anyone you know? Life is hard; everyone has problems. Some have more problems than others. According to our verse we need to have sympathy and try to help others if we can. The most important part of this verse though is towards the end.

We must be forgiving of each other in the same way God has done for us. What does that mean? Think about what God did for us. He sent His only Son to earth, to live and die for US! Because of what Jesus did by becoming the sacrifice for our sins, we are made right with God. So, if God can do such a HUGE thing for us, shouldn't we make an effort to forgive others?

I know this is what God expects, and it isn't always easy, but if we can just get to this point, we will be blessed.

Pursue the Lamb

1 Peter 3:8-9

Finally, all of you, be like minded, be sympathetic, love one another, be compassionate and humble. Do not repay evil with evil or insult with insult. On the contrary, repay evil with blessing, because to this you were called so that you may inherit a blessing.

Colossians 3:12-13

Therefore, as God's chosen people, holy and dearly loved, clothe yourselves with compassion, kindness, humility, gentleness and patience. Bear with each other and forgive one another if any of you has a grievance against someone. Forgive as the Lord forgave you.

Matthew 6:14

For if you forgive others when they sin against you, your heavenly Father will also forgive you.

Perfecting Holiness

2 Corinthians 7:1

Therefore, since we have these promises, dear friends, let us purify ourselves from everything that contaminates the body and spirit, perfecting holiness out of reverence for God.

First off, "these promises" that are mentioned, are found in the previous chapter. God has told the people (us) that He would live with us, walk among us and be our God and we would be His people. He says we will be sons and daughters of His! Those are promises from our Father.

So, because He is our Father and loves us and wants to be with us, we, out of reverence for Him, should strive to be holy! But what does that look like?

Our verse today says we need to purify ourselves of everything that contaminates our body and spirit. Think about things like alcohol abuse, overeating, drugs, anything that affects your body in an unhealthy way. For things that affect your spirit, consider things like, bitterness, unforgiveness, hatred, gossip. I'm sure you are getting the point.

Take a moment to look at your life today. Is there something you need to get rid of so you can run this race? Let your Father show you how to lighten that load and get one step closer to perfecting holiness.

Pursue the Lamb

Hebrews 12:14

Make every effort to live in peace with everyone and to be holy; without holiness no one will see the Lord.

1 Thessalonians 4:7

For God did not call us to be impure, but to live a holy life.

Colossians 1:22

But now he has reconciled you by Christ's physical body through death to present you holy in his sight, without blemish and free from accusation...

Grace of God

Galatians 2:21

I do not set aside the grace of God, for if righteousness could be gained through the law, Christ died for nothing.

Four very sad words end that verse. Christ died for nothing. I know that's not true, but you must understand what comes before that. Don't we sometimes try to do and be the best we can? Don't we follow all the rules, volunteer, feed the homeless, work hard and think, if I just do enough, it will be enough?

Beware! That is faulty thinking. Your righteousness cannot be gained through what you do! No matter what you do, it will never be enough. The apostle Paul, in our verse today, says, "Do not set aside the grace of God." That grace is the only thing that will be enough. Ephesians 2:8-9 says, "For it is by grace you have been saved, through faith-and this is not from yourselves, it is the gift of God - not by works, so that no one can boast." God gave you grace in sending His Son, Jesus, to make you good enough to go to heaven. Acceptance of Jesus makes you ready. Christ didn't die for nothing. He died for you!

Pursue the Lamb

Galatians 3:21

Is the law, therefore, opposed to the promises of God? Absolutely not! For if a law had been given that could impart life, then righteousness would certainly have come by the law.

Romans 8:1-3

Therefore, there is now no condemnation for those who are in Christ Jesus, because through Christ Jesus the law of the Spirit who gives life has set you free from the law of sin and death. For what the law was powerless to do because it was weakened by the sinful nature, God did by sending his own Son in the likeness of sinful humanity to be a sin offering.

Preparing for Battle

Psalm 144:1

Praise be to the LORD my Rock, who trains my hands for war, my fingers for battle.

When you live near a military base you learn rather quickly that there is a lot of training going on. The new recruits are practicing maneuvers over and over that may one day save their lives. They practice or train until it becomes rote or muscle memory for them, because in the heat of battle, they may not have time to sit and think about their situation.

Now, apply that to our Christian life. God is preparing and training us so that when life's battles hit us, we are so well trained we know what to do! Ephesians 6 tells us to put on the full armor of God because our fight is not against flesh and blood. We must learn to stand firm with our armor all in place to not be fooled by our enemy who goes around looking for someone to devour.

Sometimes events happen in our lives that knock the stuffing out of us, but if we have allowed God to train us, drill us and prepare us, we will come through the battle and be overcomers. Then we will be left standing on the Rock!

Pursue the Lamb

Genesis 49:24

But his bow remained steady, his strong arms stayed limber, because of the hand of the Mighty One of Jacob, because of the Shepherd, the Rock of Israel.

Ephesians 6:13

Therefore put on the full armor of God, so that when the day of evil comes, you may be able to stand your ground and after you have done everything, to stand.

Matthew 7:25

The rain came down, the streams rose, and the winds blew and beat against that house; yet it did not fall, because it had its foundation on the rock.

Be Devoted

Romans 12:10

Be devoted to one another in love. Honor one another above yourselves.

What if we started off this new day doing what this verse says? What would that look like? Would it change our world? How can we make these things be something that we put into action? These next few verses may help spur us on to being able to do just that!

Ephesians 4:32 says, "Be kind and compassionate to one another, forgiving each other, just as in Christ, God has forgiven you."

Colossians 3:12 says, "Therefore, as God's chosen people, holy and dearly loved, clothe yourselves with compassion, kindness, humility, gentleness and patience.

Did you catch it? Did you see the things the writers listed? Kindness, compassion, forgiveness, humility, gentleness, patience. These are the things that will make a difference in our lives today! They will be instrumental in helping us love others and honor them above ourselves. Let's all give it a try and see what happens!

Pursue the Lamb

Philippians 2:3-4

Do nothing out of selfish ambition or vain conceit. Rather, in humility value others above yourselves, not looking to your own interests but each of you to the interests of others.

1 Peter 1:22

Now that you have purified yourselves by obeying the truth so that you have sincere love for each other, love one another deeply from the heart.

Hebrews 13:1

Keep on loving one another as brothers and sisters.

The Perfect Law

James 1:25

But those who look intently into the perfect law that gives freedom, and continue in it-not forgetting what they have heard, but doing it-they will be blessed in what they do.

Is there such a thing as a perfect law? Let me just answer that by saying, "NO", not by human standards for sure!

What I love about today's verse is that God's law IS perfect. His word will guide you, it will lead you through life. Even better, instead of inhibiting you, like some would believe, it actually brings you freedom.

If you look intently into His Word you will be blessed. Study it, think about it, pray over it, look for other verses that tie into it. Oh my, the blessings God has for us! Most of the time these won't be material blessings, but spiritual blessings that only He can give.

The last part of the verse points us to one other idea. Once we have looked into the perfect law and we see what it is that God expects of us, then we must DO what it says. Freedom and blessing are found in obedience. He's got something just for you today. Look intently.

Pursue the Lamb

Psalm 119:34

Give me understanding, so that I may keep your law and obey it with all my heart.

Psalm 19:7

The law of the LORD is perfect, refreshing the soul. The statutes of the LORD are trustworthy, making wise the simple.

John 8:32

"Then you will know the truth and the truth will set you free."

Promote Peace

Proverbs 12:20

Deceit is in the hearts of those who plot evil, but those who promote peace have joy.

Those who promote peace have joy! One version says those who *plan* peace have joy. That means we have a choice to make, doesn't it? We can plot evil like the first part of the verse says, or we can *plan* to make peace.

Jesus, himself, said in Matthew 5:9: "Blessed are the peacemakers for they will be called children of God." People who "plan" peace will be joyful because they are following and listening to their Father.

God gives us joy because we are His kids. He wants us to promote peace, not dissension. Isaiah 26:3 says: "You will keep in perfect peace those whose minds are steadfast, because they trust in you." Trust in God today; plan peace.

Be a planner and not a plotter. Think about that today.

Pursue the Lamb

Romans 14:19

Let us therefore make every effort to do what leads to peace and to mutual edification.

Romans 12:18

If it is possible, as far as it depends on you, live at peace with everyone.

Psalm 34:14

Turn from evil and do good; seek peace and pursue it.

2 Timothy 2:22

Flee the evil desires of youth and pursue righteousness, faith, love and peace, along with those who call on the Lord out of a pure heart.

Reflections

Proverbs 27:19

As water reflects the face, so one's life reflects the heart.

I love seeing a pond or lake with the water so still that you can see the reflection of the surrounding countryside. It's beautiful, isn't it? So peaceful, so quiet. But what happens when a little wind blows across the water? You and I know, it stirs the water and distorts the picture that was so perfect earlier.

Does that ever happen in our lives? Things are going along so perfectly and bam, some event comes along and totally destroys that beautiful, serene picture.

This verse tells us that when bad things happen in our lives, how we handle those hardships, tell people what we are really made of. If we're living for God, following Him and listening to Him, they should see a great reflection. Be aware that sometimes it takes a bit of time for the waters to settle down. Trust God and He will calm the waters. If He does not calm the actual storm that is raging outside, He will calm us on the inside. Then our reflections will show the One who deserves all the praise.

Pursue the Lamb

1 John 1:6-7

If we claim to have fellowship with him and yet walk in the darkness, we lie and do not live out the truth. But if we walk in the light, as he is in the light, we have fellowship with one another, and the blood of Jesus, his Son, purifies us from all sin.

Matthew 5:8

Blessed are the pure in heart, for they will see God.

Proverbs 15:13

A happy heart makes the face cheerful, but heartache crushes the spirit.

Luke 8:24

The disciples went and woke him, saying, "Master, Master, we're going to drown!" He got up and rebuked the wind and the raging waters; the storm subsided, and all was calm.

Rooted in Prayer

1 Thessalonians 5:17 Amp

Be unceasing and persistent in prayer.

Don't give up! Don't do it! Be unceasing and persistent. That means don't ever stop. In Luke 18:2-8 Jesus tells his disciples a story. It's the story of a widow who kept going to a judge and asking him for help. She didn't have any family to help her get justice, so she set out to get legal help.

In the story, this widow woman kept going back time after time to see the judge. She went back so many times that the judge got tired of seeing her and hearing her. In other words, she bugged him till she got what she wanted!

The judge in this story wasn't necessarily a righteous man but he granted her what she asked for. We, however, have a very Righteous Judge who will answer our prayers. God doesn't have to be badgered to answer His children, but He does want us to be persistent and believe He will do what we ask.

Don't give up! Don't do it. Be persistent in your prayer life. Ask, seek and knock. Believe Jesus will do what is best for you!

Pursue the Lamb

Luke 18:1

Then Jesus told his disciples a parable to show them that they should always pray and not give up.

Romans 12:12

Be joyful in hope, patient in affliction, faithful in prayer.

Ephesians 6:18

And pray in the Spirit on all occasions with all kinds of prayers and requests. With this in mind, be alert and always keep on praying for all the Lord's people.

Luke 18:4-5

For some time he refused. But finally he said to himself, "Even though I don't fear God or care what people think, yet because this widow keeps bothering me, I will see that she gets justice, so that she won't eventually come and attack me."

Fix your Thoughts on Jesus

Hebrews 12:2a

Fixing our eyes on Jesus, the pioneer and perfector of faith.

When reading the Bible, I sometimes come across a phrase that just keeps popping out. Oh, it may be worded a bit differently, but the meaning is the same. That is what happened with today's verse. "Fix your eyes on Jesus." This was the phrase. Not only did I keep reading it in the Bible, I kept hearing it in sermons, reading it in devotional books, etc.

When God keeps putting something in front of you over and over, there must be a reason. In my case, there were some things that were about to happen that I needed to be prepared for. We don't always know what is going to happen in our lives, but God does! He can and will give you something to hang on to during the tough times. Or perhaps it will be something that is a comfort to you in a situation you are already in.

Thank God for His Word. It is hard to make it in this world without His help. Ask Him today to give you something to hang on to from His Word. In the meantime, fix your eyes and your thoughts on Jesus.

Pursue the Lamb

Micah 7:7

As for me, I watch in hope for the LORD, I wait for God my Savior; my God will hear me.

Psalm 27:8

When you said, "Seek My face," my heart said to you, "Your face, LORD, I will seek."

2 Corinthians 4:18

So we fix our eyes not on what is seen, but on what is unseen, since what is seen is temporary, but what is unseen is eternal.

Tears in a Bottle

Psalm 56:8 NLT

"You keep track of all my sorrows. You have collected all my tears in your bottle. You have recorded each one in your book."

Are you a crier? You know; one of those people who cry when they see someone else even begin to tear up? I am! I can cry at the drop of a hat! I cry when I'm leaving for a trip, at weddings, at baptisms, when I'm watching a sad movie. I think you get the picture. I don't know why I do this; if it's my empathic heart, or something else, but I do know that I like this verse. I jokingly say that instead of a bottle, God must have a jug with my name on it!

What I like about this verse is that those tears are not wasted. God made us to be feeling people. He is collecting my tears and your tears. The awesome part is that He counts them all. Every single one of them mean something to Him. He is keeping a record of each and every one. This gives me hope that things that happen to me are important to God too. This gives me comfort.

Pursue the Lamb

2 Kings 20:4-5

Before Isaiah had left the middle court, the word of the LORD came to him; "Go back and tell Hezekiah, the ruler of my people, 'This is what the LORD, the God of your father David, says: I have heard your prayer and seen your tears; I will heal you. On the third day from now you will go up to the temple of the Lord.' "

Psalm 126: 5-6

Those who sow with tears will reap with songs of joy. Those who go out weeping, carrying seed to sow, will return with songs of joy, carrying sheaves with them.

Isaiah 25:8

He will swallow up death forever. The Sovereign LORD will wipe away the tears from all faces; he will remove his people's disgrace from all the earth. The LORD has spoken.

Revelation 7:17

For the Lamb at the center of the throne will be their shepherd; he will lead them to springs of living water. And God will wipe away every tear from their eyes.

Good Friday, but what about Saturday?

John 19:30

When he had received the drink, Jesus said, "It is finished." With that, he bowed his head and gave up his spirit.

Jesus has died. This was Friday, and we know what happened on Sunday, but what do you suppose was going on during the day on Saturday? Let's think about the disciple John - he was one of Jesus' closest friends, after all he was one of the three on the Mount of Transfiguration and Jesus included him in other important miracles as well.

To John, this day of death must have brought many emotions. I'm sure on this Saturday he was grieving. Shock and denial, pain and guilt, anger, depression and loneliness were just a few of the emotions running through his head and his heart.

John had given up a lot to follow this Jesus, who is now gone! He had no job, no direction, probably no money and very little hope.

But John chose to linger near where Jesus' body was laid. And because he did, he got to see the biggest and best miracle of all!! He got to see the empty tomb and John 20:8 says, "He saw, and he believed." He knew in his heart that Jesus had risen from the dead! Hallelujah, we can have that same belief!

Saturday must have been an exhausting day of emotions, but Sunday.... Sunday was a glorious day not only for John the disciple, but for us too! Linger near where Jesus is, you won't be disappointed.

Thank You Jesus for Your sacrifice. Praise God for His resurrection power!

Pursue the Lamb

Matthew 17:1-2
After six days Jesus took with him, Peter, James and John the brother of James and led them up a high mountain by themselves. There he was transfigured before them. His face shone like the sun and his clothes became as white as the light.

Mark 16:14
Later Jesus appeared to the Eleven as they were eating; he rebuked them for their lack of faith and their stubborn refusal to believe those who had seen him after he had risen.

Luke 24: 17-19
He asked them, "What are you discussing together as you walk along?" They stood still, their faces downcast. One of them, Cleopas, asked him, "Are you only a visitor to Jerusalem and do not know the things that have happened there in these days?" "What things?" he asked.

"About Jesus of Nazareth," they replied. "He was a prophet, powerful in work and deed before God and all the people."

The Spirit will Rest on Him

Isaiah 11:2

The Spirit of the LORD will rest on Him…

We will probably not ever be a witness to a scene like what John the Baptist described in Matthew 3:16. He actually got to see the Spirit of God descend and He took the form of a dove. This dove landed on Jesus and then John heard God's Voice!

Can you imagine that scene? I'm sure it was probably a bit overwhelming. Have you ever felt the Spirit of the Lord move in your life? It can be inspiring and awesome! In Isaiah the Scripture tells us what happened when the Spirit of the Lord came upon Jesus. He gained wisdom and understanding and many more things!

Do you think there may be something here for us to learn? If we let God's Holy Spirit work in our lives, I believe we will see great and wonderful things happen. If we want more knowledge of Jesus, we must ask the Holy Spirit to help us. If we want His counsel about a problem or issue, we can ask the Holy Spirit what we should do.

Let's let Him lead and guide us every day.

Let the Spirit rest on you too.

Pursue the Lamb

Isaiah 61:1

The Spirit of the Sovereign LORD is on me, because the LORD has anointed me to proclaim good news to the poor. He has sent me to bind up the broken hearted, to proclaim freedom for the captives and release from darkness for the prisoners....

Matthew 3:16-17

As soon as Jesus was baptized he went up out of the water. At that moment heaven was opened and he saw the Spirit of God descending like a dove and alighting on him. And a voice from heaven said, "This is my Son, whom I love; with him I am well pleased."

Luke 4: 18-19

"The Spirit of the Lord is on me, because he has anointed me to proclaim good news to the poor. He has sent me to proclaim freedom for the prisoners and recovery of sight for the blind, to set the oppressed free, to proclaim the year of the Lord's favor."

Clean the Cup

Matthew 23:26

Blind Pharisee! First clean the inside of the cup and dish, and then the outside will also be clean.

I just hate it when I pull a glass or mug from the dishwasher and somehow it hasn't gotten clean on the inside. I'm not sure just how that happens, but it reminds me of our verse today.

Jesus is talking to the teachers of the law and the Pharisees. What He is seeing is their outward appearance with their robes and their tassels. He is watching how they act in public, and He is not happy with them.

He tells them to "clean the inside of the cup." In other words, work on your insides! He wants them to make sure they are living right and have their hearts in the right place with God.

Guess what? He's telling us the same thing! Be sure the inside of the cup is clean, then the outside will take care of itself.

Pursue the Lamb

Matthew 23:27

"Woe to you, teachers of the law and Pharisees, you hypocrites! You are like white washed tombs, which look beautiful on the outside but on the inside are full of the bones of the dead and everything unclean."

Luke 11:46

Jesus replied, "And you experts in the law, woe to you, because you load people down with the burdens they can hardly carry and you yourselves will not lift one finger to help them."

Isaiah 1:18

"Come now, let us reason together," says the LORD. "Though your sins are like scarlet, they shall be as white as snow; though they are red as crimson, they shall be like wool."

Don't be Afraid

Luke 2:10a

But the angel said to them, "Do not be afraid."

Isn't it wonderful to think about that first Christmas? Interesting that the first thing the angel of the Lord said to the shepherds was, "Do not be afraid."

It is certain that those shepherds had never seen anything like what they saw that night! Put yourself in their place. They were out in the fields with their sheep, maybe even getting ready to turn in for the night, when the glory of the Lord showed up! I picture a bright light from heaven, maybe a loud noise, certainly more than those men were used to on a calm night with their sheep. No wonder they were terrified!

Have you ever been terrified? Is something going on in your life that has you running scared? You are not alone. We all experience moments of terror, but just like when the angel of the Lord came to the shepherds with their message, we, too, don't need to be afraid. The "One" the angel came to announce did come. He was born so we don't have to be terrified. Thank you, Jesus, for being there for us, always.

Pursue the Lamb

Acts 23:11

The following night the Lord stood near Paul and said, "Take courage! As you have testified about me in Jerusalem, so you must also testify in Rome."

Matthew 14:27

But Jesus immediately said to them: "Take courage! It is I. Don't be afraid."

Daniel 10:12

Then he continued, "Do not be afraid, Daniel. Since the first day that you set your mind to gain understanding and to humble yourself before God, your words were heard and I have come in response to them."

Revelation 1:17

When I saw him, I fell at his feet as though dead. Then he placed his right hand on me and said: "Do not be afraid. I am the First and the Last."

Good News

Luke 2:10b

I bring you good news of great joy that will be for all the people.

Good news! God news! No, that is not a typo! The angel that came to those shepherds was bringing God news. They had a message for those shepherds. God was doing a miracle.

Of course, we know God started working Jesus' story long before this first Christmas, but history was being changed from this night forward. God has sent His most precious Gift to a broken world.

Let's look at what this part of verse 10 says: Jesus, that gift of God to us, is going to bring us joy. And He's not talking about just those shepherds, or just the Jewish people. He's talking about ALL of us. Jesus came for everyone. He wants us to have joy. He made a way, where there seemed to be no way! Thank you, God, for Your News and thank you for the joy you give us who believe!

Pursue the Lamb

Mark 1:15

"The time has come," he said. "The kingdom of God has come near. Repent and believe the good news!"

1 Corinthians 15:1-2

Now, brothers and sisters, I want to remind you of the gospel I preached to you, which you received and on which you have taken your stand. By this gospel you are saved, if you hold firmly to the word I preached to you. Otherwise, you have believed in vain.

Colossians 1:22-23

But now he has reconciled you by Christ's physical body through death to present you holy in his sight, without blemish and free from accusation - if you continue in your faith, established and firm, and do not move from the hope held out in the gospel. This is the gospel that you heard and that has been proclaimed to every creature under heaven, and of which I, Paul, have become a servant.

A Savior is Born

Luke 2:11

Today in the town of David a Savior has been born to you.

Why is Bethlehem called the city of David? King David was born in Bethlehem. He came from this small town. There is a correlation between David and Jesus. Jesus' lineage was from the line of David. Jesus' birth had been prophesied a long time ago. (2 Samuel 7:14-17).

So, when the angel of the Lord told the shepherds that a Savior was born there in Bethlehem, they would have known that to be a fulfillment of prophecy. The Jewish people were looking for the Messiah, and they knew what the prophesies about Him were. What a joy this must have been to those shepherds to know and be able to see this come to pass. (After they got over being terrified, of course!).

This Savior, Jesus, was born there in Bethlehem over 2000 years ago. He's here today! Just look around, seek Him; you'll see Him in a baby's face, in the kindness of a stranger, in the beauty of a flower, in the night sky. What a Savior who was born to us! Praise the Lord!

Pursue the Lamb

Psalm 89:35-37

"Once for all, I have sworn by my holiness-and I will not lie to David-that his line will continue forever and his throne endure before me like the sun; it will be established forever like the moon, the faithful witness in the sky."

2 Samuel 7:16-17

"Your house and your kingdom will endure forever before me; your throne will be established forever." Nathan reported to David all the words of this entire revelation.

Luke 1:32-33

"He will be great and will be called the Son of the Most High. The Lord God will give him the throne of his father David, and he will reign over the house of Jacob forever; his kingdom will never end."

Jeremiah 33:17

For this is what the LORD says; 'David will never fail to have a man to sit on the throne of the house of Israel.

Here's your Sign

Luke 2:12a

This will be a sign to you.

That angel of the Lord packed a lot into a few sentences. The first part of verse twelve says that the shepherds were to be given a sign.

Signs are important. They tell you which direction to go. Signs can help you stay on a path, keep you from danger, announce a happening, or even identify a place you want to go. We need signs. Well, at least I do. If it weren't for signs, I'd probably never find my way home.

Aren't you glad we have Jesus as our sign? He's always there, always helping us see our way. He's given us His Word as our direction finder, pointing out the best way to walk and to live and how to treat other people.

The sign the shepherds were given was to help them find the baby Jesus. The sign we are given is still the same one, except He's not a baby any longer! He's our Savior.

Pursue the Lamb

John 12:37

Even after Jesus had performed so many signs in their presence, they still would not believe in him.

John 20:30-31

Jesus performed many other signs in the presence of his disciples, which are not recorded in this book. But these are written that you may believe that Jesus is the Messiah, the Son of God, and that by believing you may have life in his name.

Isaiah 35:8-10

And a highway will be there; it will be called the Way of Holiness; it will be for those who walk on that Way. The unclean will not journey on it; wicked fools will not go about on it. No lion will be there , nor any ravenous beast; they will not be found there. But only the redeemed will walk there, and those the LORD has rescued will return. They will enter Zion with singing; everlasting joy will crown their heads. Gladness and joy will overtake them, and sorrow and sighing will flee away.

Baby in a Manger

Luke 2:12b

You will find a baby wrapped in cloths and lying in a manger.

I've wondered if there were other babies born that same night. I'm sure Mary wasn't the only woman expecting a baby as the people traveled to their hometowns for the census taking. I'm sure other mothers took clothing for that new baby, just in case that little one happened to make an appearance while they were traveling. That must have been a tough place to be in.

The thing that sets this story apart from others though, is where this baby ended up. He was laid in a manger or a feed trough! He was born in a barn. What a humble beginning. I'm sure those shepherds would not have felt comfortable going to an inn or a palace, but they were okay with going to a stable.

It seems that from the moment the angel appeared to the lowly shepherds, to their finding the baby lying in the manger, the message was clear. Jesus came for everyone, even the lowest.

Pursue the Lamb

Isaiah 7:14

Therefore the LORD himself will give you a sign: The virgin will conceive and give birth to a son, and will call him Immanuel.

Luke 2:6-7

While they were there, the time came for the baby to be born, and she gave birth to her firstborn, a son. She wrapped him in cloths and placed him in a manger, because there was no guest room available to them.

Luke 1:42

In a loud voice she exclaimed: "Blessed are you among women, and blessed is the child you will bear!"

The Messiah

Luke 2:11b

He is the Messiah, the Lord.

Messiah, the Chosen One or the Anointed One. This Messiah was expected for a long time. People had waited and waited for Him to come, and there were various reasons. Some thought He would be a military leader and help get them out from under the thumb of Rome.

Others thought He would come to heal them and make their lives easier. But God had a more eternal idea in mind.

You see, He knew that we needed spiritual help. We needed someone to stand in our place for the sins we've committed. The only One who could do that was Jesus. He was the Perfect One. He still is. He has stood in our place on the cross and taken every sin and abolished it forever. I hope He is your Messiah and Lord today.

Pursue the Lamb

1 Timothy 4:10

That is why we labor and strive, because we have put our hope in the living God, who is the Savior of all people, and especially of those who believe.

1 John 4:14

And we have seen and testify that the Father has sent his Son to be the Savior of the world.

Acts 2:36

Therefore let all Israel be assured of this: God has made this Jesus, whom you crucified, both Lord and Messiah.

Acts 3:19-20

Repent, then, and turn to God, so that your sins may be wiped out, that times of refreshing may come from the Lord, and that he may send the Messiah, who has been appointed for you— even Jesus.

www.ingramcontent.com/pod-product-compliance
Lightning Source LLC
Chambersburg PA
CBHW050442150626
46551CB00028B/1111